SUMMER CAMP
@Home
HANDBOOK

Volume One

SUMMER CAMP HANDBOOK

5 Weeks of Camp Themes & Activities

Lora Langston

2018

Summer Camp at Home Handbook

Camp Muddy Socks, Volume One

Want to be the coolest parental unit on the block? Whether you're a neighborhood caregiver, homeschooler, youth group director, a member of a co-op, or stay at home with your kids during the summer, give kids the experience of summer camp- at home!

Keep it simple, fun, and engaging. After 15 years of child care and directing summer camps, we know a thing or two about planning activities and the time commitments needed to keep kids happy.

Fun, engaging camps are broken up into small sections of time. The best part of doing camp on your own at home is you can shorten or lengthen the schedule as needed. If an activity doesn't connect with kids, that's okay! Move on to an activity from our alternative schedule. Each camp theme comes with a monthly planner. Be sure to prep in advance.

Many non-profit organizations offer outreach programs for groups at no cost or minimal cost. You'll need to call and schedule in advance to get the dates you want. Look to museums, parks, and even libraries for special enrichment programming. Do a search for "summer outreach" in your area.

In case you want to make it more official, we've included everything you need to organize, plan, and facilitate camp at home! You'll find registration forms, payment forms, sample letters to camper's parents, waivers, allergy and intake forms, and daily schedules. With all of this information, you'll be able to launch your own official summer camp with 5 action packed weeks!

Tip: Don't have a yard that will work for summer camp? Try a local park with clean restrooms and a free shelter.

Happy Camping!

CONTENTS

Daily Welcome & Camp Starter
- Song: Welcome Song
- Camp Pledge & Motto
- Intro: Icebreaker Game

It's all Rainbows
- Song
- Snacks
- Arts & Crafts
- Science
- Get Moving
- Enrichment

Silly Spaghetti
- Song
- Snacks
- Arts & Crafts
- Science
- Get Moving
- Enrichment

Eat Worms
- Song
- Snacks
- Arts & Crafts
- Science
- Get Moving
- Enrichment

Do Monkey Around
- Song
- Snacks
- Arts & Crafts
- Science
- Get Moving
- Enrichment

Sharks vs. Chickens
- Song
- Snacks
- Arts & Crafts
- Science
- Get Moving
- Enrichment

Additional Daily Time Fillers
- More Camp Snacks & Edible Art
- Edible Paint Recipes
- Fun Science Activities
- Group Games
- Get Kids Moving Activities

Forms & Registrations
- Typical Schedule (Sample)
- Printable Daily Activity Schedule
- Printable Snack Menu
- Blank Calendar
- Printable Birthday Poster
- Sample Parent Letter
- Sample Camp Flyer
- Camp Registration Forms
    - Weekly Camper Registration
    - Waivers
    - Medical/Allergy Info Sheet
    - Photo/Media Permission

Welcome & Camp Starter

Daily Welcome & Camp Starter
- Song: Welcome Song
- *Camp Muddy Socks* Pledge
- Intro: Icebreaker Game

Every camp needs a motto, a pledge, and a flag. The first day of camp, teach campers the *Camp Muddy Socks* motto and pledge.

Camp Flag:

Grab some inexpensive white pillow cases and fabric paint and hold a design contest for the camp flag. It's a good idea to have campers design their ideas on paper first. Once completed, vote by secret ballot. Attach the winning flag design to the end of a broomstick and stick it in the ground to welcome guests to camp.

Camp Pledge:

Campers stand in circle with hands on hips and one foot in center.

"I pledge to have fun, follow directions, keep my hands to myself, be kind, and not cry over muddy socks."

Camp Motto:

It's not a successful day at camp until someone gets their socks muddy!

Icebreaker Game: *Who am I?*

If you've opened up your camp to the neighborhood, to the extended community, or just want to break the ice, this game is a great way to get everyone into the camp groove.

Time:
Approx. 15 minutes

Materials Needed:
Sticky Note Paper, Markers

Steps:
On a sticky note, write the name of a famous animated character.

Suggested characters include: Mickey Mouse, Elmo, Spongebob, Charlie Brown, Snoopy, Dora the Explorer, Steve from Minecraft, Homer Simpson, Mario, Yoshi, Cat in the Hat, & Pikachu.

Camp leader sticks a sticky note onto each camper's back.

Campers move throughout the circle asking each other questions.

Players are allowed to ask each person a yes or no question.

The person asked must respond with only a yes or no.

Sample questions include: "Am I a kid?" "Do I wear a red hat?" "Am I girl?" "Am I a boy?"

Play continues until each player solves the mystery of "Who am I?"

It's all Rainbows

It's all Rainbows (Designed for campers 6-16.)

Planning Calendar

Song:
- *Rainbow Trails*

Snacks:
- Rainbow Slush
- Rainbow Sandwiches

Games:
- Balloon Volleyball
- Balloon Stomp
- Jump to the End of the Rainbow

Arts & Crafts:
- Rainbow Coasters

Science:
- Prism Rainbows
- Rainbow Stacking Liquids

Enrichment:
- *Rainbow Stew Skit*
- Plan a Field Trip to a Weather Station.

SUN	MON	TUES	WED	THURS	FRI	SAT

Song to Sing: *Rainbow Trails* (Sung to *Jingle Bells* Tune)
Companion Activity:
Read *It's Raining* and *Weather Forecasting* by Gail Gibbons

Rainbow Trails, Rainbow Trails, Rainbow here today
Oh what fun it is to slide down a rainbow all the way. Hey!

Rainbow Trails, Rainbow Trails, Rainbow here today
Oh what fun it is to slide down a rainbow all the way!

Splashing through the rain, on a rainbow slide of gold
Down the slide we go, laughing all the way

Ha ha ha!

Rainbow Trails Rainbow Trails, Rainbow here today
Oh what fun it is to slide down a rainbow all the way

Rainbow Trails Rainbow Trails, Rainbow here today
Oh what fun it is to slide down a rainbow all the way

Colors on Rainbows shine making it so bright
What fun it is to slide and sing on a rainbow slide today

Rainbow Trails Rainbow Trails, Rainbow here today
Oh what fun it is to slide down a rainbow all the way. Hey!

Rainbow Trails Rainbow Trails, Rainbow here today
Oh what fun it is to slide down a rainbow all the way

Theme Snack: Rainbow Slush

Time:
Approx. 35 minutes

Materials Needed:
24 Freezer Pops, Whipped Topping, Large Glass Bowl, Rubber Spatula, Glass

Steps:
Freeze pops.

Choose clear glass dish. (Trifle bowls work nicely.)

Pop dish into freezer to chill.

Sort pops by color.

Choose one color, leave rest in freezer or ice chest to chill.

Start with bottom layer, darkest color first.

While still sealed in wrapper, crush pop with bottom of glass.

Cut open pop.

Remove glass trifle dish from freezer.

Pour crushed pop pieces into glass dish.

Smooth with a plastic spatula.

Between layers, place glass dish back into freezer to chill for 5 minutes.

Repeat with each color.

When layers are complete, spread whipped topping on top.

To serve, cut like cake.

Tip: Sing *Rainbow Trails* song while individual layers chill.

Theme Snack: Rainbow Graham Crackers

Time:
Approx. 25 minutes

Materials Needed:
Box of Graham Crackers, 2 Cups Milk, Add Food Coloring to Vanilla Pudding or use Packages of Pudding in Red, Orange, Purple, Blue, Green, and Yellow, Whipped Topping, Rainbow Sprinkles

Steps:

Per package directions, beat pudding mix and milk together until smooth.

If not using separate colored pudding, divide into six individual bowls.

Add food coloring and blend.

Spread one color onto 1/2 graham square.

Place ½ graham square on top to make a sandwich.

Spread next color on top of sandwich.

Repeat using all colors.

Spread whipped cream on top layer of sandwich.

Add rainbow sprinkles.

Chill.

Serve cold.

Tip: Between layers, talk about color wheel.

Get Moving: Balloon Volleyball

Time:
Approx. 30 minutes

Materials Needed:
Variety pack of Large Balloons

Steps:

Blow up a variety of rainbow colored balloons.

Locate a divider line to serve as net (jump rope, masking tape.)

Choose 1 referee for each team.

Keep score for opposing team.

Players hit balloons back and forth across net until someone misses.

When one team misses balloon, the other team scores 1 point.

The first team to reach 10 points wins.

Get Moving: Balloon Stomp

Time:
Approx. 15 minutes

Materials Needed:
Variety of Large Balloons, Curling Ribbon, Scissors, Grass Paint

Steps:
Blow up a variety of rainbow colored balloons, paint large circle in grass approx. 30' in diameter.

Give one balloon to each player with 2' of curling ribbon.

Players blow up their own balloon.

Tie one balloon to each player's ankle.

Tell player's they must stay inside circle.

Camp leader counts to 3.

On 3, each player tries to stomp other player's balloons.

The last person with balloon intact wins.

Get Moving: Jump to the End of the Rainbow

Time:
Approx. 20 minutes

Materials Needed:
Masking Tape or 2 Jump Ropes, Bubble Wrap, Small Yellow Paper Party Plates, (3 per Player) Permanent Markers, Rainbow Party Decoration

Steps:
Find an area to measure 8' in a straight line.

If using bubble wrap, spread it the length of line. (A roll of garbage bags also works.) Mark start line with masking tape.

Place rainbow decoration at finish line.

Before play, each camper writes their name on 3 small yellow plates.

One at a time, each player stands at one end of marked area.

Like a long jumper, with feet together, player swings arms back and jumps forward as far as he can.

Leprechauns use magic to boost their jumps.

Tell each player to think positively as they prepare to jump.

See if they can find their inner magic to jump further each time.

Player marks spot where back of his heel lands by placing a coin on ground. Camp leader measures distance from the start line to coin.

Player who jumps furthest wins, but keep focus on improving personal best.

Arts & Crafts: Rainbow Coasters

Time:
Approx. 30 minutes

Materials Needed:
30 Red Pony Beads, 24 Orange Pony Beads, 18 Yellow Pony Beads, 12 Green Pony Beads, 5 Blue Pony Beads, 1 Purple Pony Bead, 4" x 1 ¼" Round Cake Pan, Muffin Pan, or Cookie Sheet with Cookie Cutter

Steps:
Starting with red on outer edge, arrange pony beads with holes up in descending order toward center of pan.

Bake at 400 degrees for 15 to 20 minutes.

Bake beads for different amounts of time to get different results.

Let cool, pop out of pan.

For visual steps visit:
https://www.kidscreativechaos.com/2014/04/girl-scout-activity-pony-bead-rainbow.html

Tip: Use plastic circle templates and Perler (Fuse) Beads with an iron.

Science Activity: Prism Rainbows

Time:
Approx. 15 minutes

Materials Needed:
Small Prisms, Sunlight, Incandescent Light, Fluorescent Light, Note Paper

Steps:
Hold small prism with one finger at top and one finger at bottom. Position the prism 3" in front of eye. Look through one side of prism in direction of light source.

With prism, look at incandescent lamp. What colors do you see?

With prism, look at fluorescent lamp. What colors do you see?

With prism, look at sunlight. What colors do you see?

Record observations on note paper- list colors in order from left to right.

Roy G. Biv. Do you see all the colors of the rainbow?

(red, orange, yellow, green, blue, indigo, violet)

Are there differences with each light source?

Are colors in the same order?

Are colors the same shape?

Science Activity: Rainbow Stacking Liquids

Time: Approx. 30 minutes

Materials Needed:
Food Coloring, Clear Glass Cylinder (Tall Drinking Glass), Colored Lamp Oil, Turkey Baster, Plastic Cups, Light Corn Syrup, Water, Vegetable Oil, Blue *Dawn* Dish Liquid Soap, Rubbing Alcohol, Honey

Steps:
Before you start, make sure it works by reading instructions carefully. The details are very important. All steps must be done in order.

Measure and Color it!
Measure each liquid and place into an individual plastic cup. You'll have 7 total. Use 6-12 oz. of each. The size of your glass may call for more or less. To insure it works, use exact same amount of each liquid.

Pour it!
Liquids MUST be layered in order. Start at bottom of glass and work toward top.

- *Honey* - Amber
- *Corn Syrup* (Add food coloring of your choice.)
- *Dish Soap* - Blue
- *Water* - Clear (Add food coloring of your choice.)
- *Vegetable Oil* - Yellow
- *Rubbing Alcohol* (Add food coloring of your choice.)
- *Lamp Oil* - (Choose your favorite color.)

Pour Slowly: As you pour each color into cylinder, be careful not to touch the sides. If you do, wipe off with dry paper towel.

Honey, Corn Syrup, Dish Soap: Let each layer settle before adding next layer.

Water: Use turkey baster to layer on water. Now, liquids can touch sides of glass. Using baster, hold it on inside wall of glass and slowly squeeze. Water should slowly trickle down inside of glass. Continue until layer is complete.

Vegetable Oil: Rinse turkey baster with warm water. Fill with vegetable oil. Use same method of trickle down that you did in water step above.

Rubbing Alcohol: Now, wash turkey baster with warm soap and water. Fill with rubbing alcohol. Use same method of trickle down that you did in water step above.

Lamp Oil: Once again, wash turkey baster with warm soap and water. Fill baster with lamp oil, keep finger over tip. Use same method of trickle down that you did in water step above. (Remember, lamp oil is flammable. Keep away from stove or open flame.)

Tip: Take photo and empty glass quickly, you don't want anyone to take a sip!

Rainbow Stew

RAINBOW STEW

written by Lora Langston
Copyright (c) 2012

CAST OF CHARACTERS

LUCKY
LINDY
LAWRY
LOUIE

CHRIS
PATTY
SAM

EVERYONE ELSE

LINDY(#2)
picks up and smells gold, wrinkles nose
Eww, rotten, chocolate milk.

leprechauns look at each other, crinkle faces, and make gagging motions

#1 fans in front of face
#2 pretends to stick finger down throat
#3 leprechaun enters stage left

LAWRY(#3)
Mmm, Mmm, Mmm, something smells yummy?

#1 & #2 look at each other wide-eyed

LAWRY(#3)
Can I have a taste?

LUCKY(#1)
shrugs shoulders, puts arms out to side

I guess... If you really want to.
grabs shovel and digs in

LINDY
fights to get shovel from #3/Larry
No! It's not done. If you eat it now, we'll never see the rainbow.

LAWRY
handing over the shovel
Rainbow stew? Why didn't you say so? That'll be worth the wait.

leprechauns continue stirring and taking turns tasting
#4 enters stage left

LOUIE (#4)
Whaaatcha doin'?

LUCKY, LINDY, LAWRY
shout in unison
Making rainbow stew!

LOUIE
You're going to catch a human?
crumples up face

LUCKY
walks over to Louie, places arm around him, winks
I'm going to catch a bunch of humans. This is my best stew yet.

LINDY
jumps up and down, clapping
I can't wait for the trickery to begin.

LAWRY
rubbing tummy
I can't wait to eat it!

LOUIE
slaps forehead
I can't wait to watch you all making fools of yourselves.

LINDY
sniffs air again
Smells like it's done.

LOUIE
(think grumpy dwarf, speak sarcastically)
Smells like chocolate and flowers.
peers into pot

LUCKY
Exactly!
picks up piece of gold, savors scent, then furiously begins throwing gold out of pot

LINDY
peers into pot
(shrieks) I see it!
digs into pot and pulls out rainbow switching hands as he digs, stretches end to tree/pole across room

LUCKY
starts doing jumping jacks
(speaks giddily, singing) I'm so excited! And I just can't hide it!

LOUIE
(sarcastic, monotone, like a robot)
I'm about to lose control. I think I like it.
gathers gold, fills pot

LINDY
Shh! Get down! I hear humans.
looks from side to side

LUCKY
looks around nervously, runs around in circles like a ninny, knocking all leprechauns to the ground

Everyone drops and covers with shamrock leaves

LAWRY
(Giggling)
Here they come. Look at them, they look silly in those clothes with that plain hair and ugly shoes. Where's their sense of style?

LOUIE
pulling on Lawry's hair
(speaks in monotone) Yes. They should be on "*What Not to Wear*."
(shouting) Get down! Are you trying to get caught? If a human kid catches you, he'll keep you in a shoebox!

humans enter stage right, giggling & skipping, touching the rainbow

LOUIE
Oh, Nacho chips! Look at them touching our rainbow with those germ infested, pudgy human fingers.

All leprechauns scramble to cover Louie's mouth
(Unison) Shh! Shh! Shh!

humans are giggly and noisy, unaware of the outburst. They stop center stage and speak

CHRIS (HUMAN #1)
looking around

Do you believe in leprechauns?

PATTY (HUMAN #2)
I hope they aren't real. I heard they are nasty little creatures.

SAM (HUMAN #3)
I think they just have a good sense of humor.

LOUIE
(whispering with sarcasm) Do you believe in humans?

others shove him away, gesture for quiet

CHRIS
holds stomach
I'm starting to feel sick to my stomach.

PATTY
leans over in pain
I know me too. Do I smell chocolate?
sniffs air

SAM
Smells like rotten milk to me.

CHRIS
sniffs air
I smell that but... what else is it? Dirty Diapers?
leprechauns grumble from their hiding place

PATTY
Are you kidding me? I heard leprechauns smell like dirty diapers!
(All leprechauns shout) The gold!

PATTY
I think it's a leprechaun trap. Did you hear that?

CHRIS
(to Patty) I thought I heard tiny voices shouting gold. What should we do?

SAM
Run!
Sam runs around shamrock pile, trips over pot of gold
Hey! Look at this. It's not a myth…

PATTY
runs over to pot and starts throwing out gold
This is amazing. But I think we better leave it alone.

CHRIS
grabs gold off the ground
Are you kidding me? This is our chance at fame and fortune.

SAM
sits down under rainbow, rocks back and forth
More like our chance to be tarred and feathered by miniature meanies.

LOUIE
throws gold at Sam

SAM
jumps up, runs to Patty, hanging on for dear life
Did you see that? I just got pelted by gold.

LOUIE
jumps out of shamrock patch
Boo! I'm gonna get you.
jumps up, grabs at him

LUCKY
Will you get back here! That isn't how you catch a human!

CHRIS
places hands on hips
Oh really? And just how do you catch a human?

LOUIE
Well, obviously a shoebox won't work.

PATTY
Why do you want to catch us?

LINDY
If a leprechaun captures a human, he gets more gold and loses his dirty diaper odor. I don't care about the gold. I want to smell like roses.

LOUIE
What do you get if you catch a leprechaun?

SAM
I guess the wealth of owning gold and a dirty diaper odor. It's like getting skunked. It's probably a defense mechanism to keep enemies at bay. By the way, I'm not afraid of you.

LOUIE
You should be; I'm a sneaky monkey. (growls)

PATTY
I think the dirty diaper odor is a lesson to you. Don't be greedy and grumpy, don't smell gross.

LAWRY
So, if I stop coveting gold, maybe I won't smell like dirty diapers anymore?

CHRIS
So, if I take the gold home, I'll be cursed with rotten egg smell?

LOUIE
You'd be getting off easy. Is it *your* gold?

CHRIS
You know its not.

PATTY
Would you rather smell like rotten eggs or go to jail?

CHRIS
hangs head
Neither. They can keep their stupid gold.

SAM
Don't worry be happy; that's what I always say.

LUCKY
I guess it's worth a try!

PATTY
And maybe your friend won't need to be so grumpy... after he stops worrying about protecting his treasure all the time.

points finger at Louie
You all need to find a real hobby. What do you do with the gold anyway?

LINDY
You mean like knitting?

LOUIE
(with sarcasm) Whatever.

LUCKY
Gold is magical. It gives us whatever we need. What would you do with gold?

CHRIS
I'd put in in the bank and save it for a rainy day.

LOUIE
Why? Rainy days bring rainbows and rainbows bring pots of gold. Don't you know anything?

SAM
Why do you hate humans?

LOUIE
(monotone voice) I thought we covered that. Humans keep leprechauns in shoeboxes.

SAM
I don't know anyone with a leprechaun in a shoebox.

CHRIS
Me neither.

PATTY
I have a cockroach in a shoebox.

EVERYONE ELSE
(grimacing) Ewwww..

Silly Spaghetti

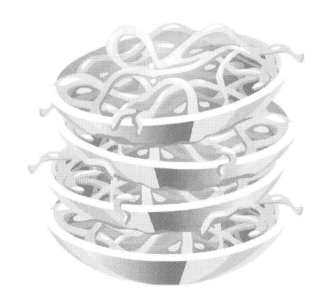

Silly Spaghetti (Designed for Campers 6-16.)

Planning Calendar

Song:
- *On Top of Spaghetti*

Snacks:
- Crunchy Spaghetti Munchies

Arts & Crafts:
- Paint with Spaghetti

Science:
- Spaghetti Strength

Get Moving Games:
- Oodles of Noodles
- Noodle Noggins

Strategy Game:
- Spaghetti Stick Towers

Enrichment:
- Play *Yeti in my Spaghetti*
- Plan a Field Trip to a *Spaghetti Factory* for Lunch
- Watch the Movie, "*Cloudy with a Chance of Meatballs*"

SUN	MON	TUES	WED	THURS	FRI	SAT

Song to Sing: *On Top of Spaghetti* (Sung to *On Top of Old Smokey* Tune)
Companion Activity:
Read and watch *Cloudy with a Chance of Meatballs*

On top of spaghetti, all covered with cheese

I lost my poor meatball when somebody sneezed

It rolled off the table, and onto the floor

And then my poor meatball rolled out of the door

It rolled down the garden, and under a bush

And then my poor meatball was nothing but mush

The mush was as tasty, as tasty could be

And the very next summer, it grew into a tree

The tree was all covered, all covered with moss

And on it grew meatballs, all covered with sauce

So if you have spaghetti, all covered with cheese

Hold onto your meatball, 'cause someone might sneeze.

Theme Snack: Crunchy Spaghetti Munchies

Time:
Approx. 25 minutes

Materials Needed:
1 lb. Spaghetti Noodles, Cooking Oil, Baking Sheet, Large Pot, Large Serving Bowl, Seasoning (Salt, ½ C. Parmesan Cheese, 2 tbsp. Oregano)

Steps:
Prepare spaghetti per package directions.

Drizzle oil onto baking sheet, set aside.

In small bowl, mix your seasoning blend, set aside.

Place drained spaghetti noodles onto prepared baking sheet.

In large pot, heat up 3" of oil.

Place noodles in pot and fry in small batches. (30 seconds to 1 min.)

Flip to get golden on both sides.

Drain each batch on paper towel.

While warm, sprinkle with seasonings.

Break into small pieces, transfer to serving bowl.

Tip: Serve with toppings like red pepper flakes, basil, and marinara for dipping.

Art: Paint with Spaghetti

Time:
Approx. 30 minutes

Materials Needed:
3 lbs. Cooked Spaghetti Noodles, Bare Feet, Styrofoam Trays or Plates, Large Rolls of Newsprint Paper or Back of Wrapping Paper Rolls, Homemade Flour or Pudding Paint (Recipe in back of book.)

Steps:

With camper's help, make edible paint.

Each painter chooses 3 colors, pours onto trays.

Roll out 5' of paper per camper.

Campers remove their shoes and socks.

Campers use feet to pick up spaghetti noodles, dip in paint, and drop on paper. Once noodles are on paper, use feet to move noodles and paint a masterpiece.

Science Activity: Spaghetti Strength
Stem Video: https://www.youtube.com/watch?v=B5q1nwDbj-4

Time:
Approx. 35 minutes

Materials Needed:
1 lb. Spaghetti Noodles, 2 sheets of Styrofoam, Wooden Building Blocks, Heavy Books, Box of Spaghetti, Scissors, String, Paperclip, Plastic Cup, Coins, Rubber Bands, Safety Goggles, Two Objects of Equal Height: Chairs, Tables, or Large Cardboard Boxes

Steps:
Investigate how much weight spaghetti can hold when in vertical position.

Discuss results.

Next, see if placing spaghetti horizontally makes a difference.

Are many pieces stronger than 1 piece?

Runs tests.

Prop spaghetti up with sheets of styrofoam.

Start with 1, then 3, then 5 and so on.

Each time, place an item on your spaghetti bridge.

What happens?

Now, try a cantilever test.

Give each camper 25 pieces of uncooked spaghetti, 30" of tape and 60" of string.

Set 2 items at equal height (like chairs.)

Leave gap between items- just a few inches less than length of spaghetti noodle.

Cut 2 small holes toward top of plastic cup, under rim, opposite from each other.

Tie string through holes in cup forming handle.

Bend paperclip into either a 'C' or 'S' shape.

Place single noodle across gap between chairs (or equal height objects of your choice.)

With paperclip hook, hang string handle on cup from strands of spaghetti.

Slowly fill your cup bucket to test strength.

Fill until noodles break.

Add more noodles (bundle with tape or rubber bands) to increase strength.

How many coins will 200 noodles hold?

Does bundling with tape hold more than bundling with rubber bands?

Tip: Experiment with different connection items and different items for weight.

Get Moving Game: Oodles of Noodles

Time:
Approx. 20 minutes

Materials Needed:
1 lb. Spaghetti Noodles, Pool Noodles, Masking Tape, Large Open Space

Steps:

Mark area with masking tape 25' from start to finish line.

Campers must walk with spaghetti noodle balanced on pool noodle.

May not touch pasta noodle while racing.

If noodle falls, stop, balance spaghetti noodle on end of pool noodle again.

Play ends when every member of one team crosses finish line.

Get Moving Game: Noodle Noggins

Time:
Approx. 15 minutes

Materials Needed:
1 lb. Spaghetti Noodles, Cooked.

Steps:

Divide campers into teams.

Select camper from each team to receive hairstyle.

Place camper in chair at opposite end of room.

Give each player cooked spaghetti noodle and line up, single file.

Camp leader claps hands to start game.

On clap, camper runs down placing spaghett on other camper's head.

Then, he runs back and tags next camper to do same.

Winner is team who successfully adds most noodles to hairstyle.

If noodles fall off, it doesn't count.

Be sure to take turns getting noggins styled.

Tip: Don't forget to take photos for parents.

Strategy Game: Spaghetti Stick Towers

Time:
Approx. 25 minutes

Materials Needed:
1 lb. Spaghetti Noodles, Mini Marshmallows, Timer, Roll of Pennies

Steps:

Divide campers into equal groups.

Give each group, ½ box of spaghetti noodles and ½ bag marshmallows.

Teams are allowed to break noodles to resize.

Set build time limit to 5-10 minutes.

Tallest Tower - Must stand for 1 minute after timer to win.

Strongest Tower - Team must build noodle platform on top.

Can the tower withstand weight?

Place coins on tower one at a time.

How many can it hold?

Tower that holds most wins.

Eat Worms

Eat Worms (Designed for Campers 6-16.)

Planning Calendar

Song:
- *Herman the Worm*

Snacks:
- Strawberry Banana Worms

Arts & Crafts:
- Make Edible Gummy Worms
- Pipe Cleaner Bead Worms

Science:
- Dancing Worms
- Make a Worm Farm

Get Moving:
- Stuck in the Mud
- Tiggy off the Ground
- Worms vs. Snakes

Silly Game:
- Slurpin' for Worms

Enrichment:
- Watch the movie, *"How to Eat Fried Worms"*

SUN	MON	TUES	WED	THURS	FRI	SAT

Song to Sing: *Herman the Worm*

Companion Activity:
Read and watch *How to Eat Fried Worms*

Sittin' on a fence post, chewin' my bubblegum
chomp chomp chomp chomp

Playin' with my yo yo
do wap do wap (pretend to use a yo yo)

When along came Herman the Worm
And he was this big (hold fingers a few inches apart)

So I said, Herman, what happened? (put arms out, shrug)
And he said, I ate my sister

Sittin' on a fence post, chewin' my bubblegum
chomp chomp chomp chomp

Playin' with my yo yo
do wap do wap (pretend to use a yo yo)

When along came Herman the worm
And he was this big (hands about six inches apart)

So I said, Herman, what happened? (put arms out, shrug)
And he said, I ate my mother

Sittin' on a fence post, chewin' my bubblegum
chomp chomp chomp chomp

Playin' with my yo yo
do wap do wap (pretend to use a yo yo)

When along came Herman the worm
And he was this big (hands about two feet apart)

So I said, Herman, what happened? (put arms out, shrug)
And he said, I ate my father

Sittin' on a fence post, chewin' my bubblegum
chomp chomp chomp chomp

Playin' with my yo yo
do wap do wap (pretend to use a yo yo)

When along came Herman the worm
And he was this big (hands as far apart as possible)

So I said, Herman, what happened? (put arms out, shrug)
And he said, I ate my grandpa

Sittin' on a fence post, chewin' my bubblegum
chomp chomp chomp chomp

Playin' with my yo yo
do wap do wap (pretend to use a yo yo)

When along came Herman the worm
And he was this big (fingers close together again)

So I said, Herman, what happened? (put arms out, shrug)
And he said, I burped!

Theme Snack: Strawberry Banana Worms

Time:
Approx. 15 minutes

Materials Needed:
Fresh Strawberries, Bananas, Vanilla Yogurt, Mini Chocolate Chips

Steps:

Slice strawberries and bananas into thin slices.

Give each camper one whole strawberry.

Have campers dip each slice into yogurt.

Arrange strawberry and banana slices into shape of worm.

Yogurt will act as glue.

Place whole strawberry in front to create head for worm.

Dip chocolate chips in yogurt.

Place two chips on whole strawberry for eyes.

Theme Snack: Homemade Gummy Worms

Time:
Approx. 30 minutes

Materials Needed:
2 Packs Strawberry Gelatin, 1 Package Unflavored Gelatin, ¾ C. Whipping Cream, 3 C. Boiling Water, Green Food Coloring, 100 Flexible Straws, Tall, Skinny Container, Rubber Band

Steps:
Combine gelatin in bowl, add boiling water.

Let cool, add whipping cream and 15 drops green food coloring.

Grab straws, stretch out flexi part, put in tall container.

Keep as many straws in container as possible for a tight fit.

Add more straws as needed to keep standing straight.

Place rubber band around straws to keep upright.

Fill straws with gelatin, let set until firm.

Use a rolling pin to roll over straws and squeeze out worms or run warm water over the straws to release gelatin gummy worms.

Art Activity: Pipe Cleaner Bead Worms

Time:

Approx. 20 minutes

Materials Needed:

Hot Glue or Tacky Glue, Pipe Cleaners, Googly Eyes, Colorful Beads

Steps:

String beads onto pipe cleaners to create worms.

Make patterns with colors of local sports teams.

Attach googly eyes with hot glue or tacky glue.

Loop the first and last bead through end of pipe cleaner and twist closed.

Science Activity: Dancing Worms

Time:

Approx. 25 minutes

Materials Needed:

Gummy Worms, Baking Soda, Vinegar, Water, Scissors, Timer, Fork

Steps:

Cut gummy worms into quarters

Fill glass with 1 C. cold water.

Measure 3 Tbs. of baking soda, stir into glass.

Mix gummy worm pieces into water.

Set timer, wait 15 minutes for worms to soak up baking soda.

Tip: Play a quick game of 20 Questions while you wait.

Fill second glass with vinegar.

When timer beeps, remove worms from glass.

One at a time, place worms into vinegar.

Worms begin to bubble and rise to surface.

Science Activity: Worm Farm

Time:
Approx. 1 hour, ongoing

Materials Needed:
Clear Plastic Bucket with Lid, Shredded Newspaper, Topsoil, Spray Bottle of Water, Worms, Food Scraps

Steps:
Shred newspaper, place in bucket.

Dampen with spray bottle as you layer into bucket.

Shovel soil into bucket.

Purchase fishing worms in advance or go on worm hunt.

Look under decks, turn over rocks and stepping stones.

Add worms to top of the farm.

Have campers save fruit and veggie scraps from lunches to feed worms.

Do this every day of camp (and as long as you have your worm farm.)

If you stop feeding them, they will die.

Circulate farm once per week.

Stir bedding around to add air pockets.

Eventually, worms will do this themselves.

Poke holes in lid, place lid on farm when not in use.

Store in cool, dry, shady spot.

At end of camp, release worms.

Get Moving Game: Stuck in the Mud

Time:
Approx. 25 minutes

Materials Needed:
Large Open Space

Steps:

'It' chases other players.

When player is tagged, he becomes "stuck in the mud," unable to move.

To free stuck player from mud, another player must crawl through stuck player's legs.

When this happens, stuck player returns to game and continues play.

Game is finished when all players are "stuck in the mud."

Player that has been stuck in mud longest becomes 'it' for next round.

Get Moving Game: Tiggy off the Ground

Time:
Approx. 25 minutes

Materials Needed:
Large Open Space, Timer

Steps:

Play starts with everyone laying on ground.

When camp leader shouts, "Go," everyone jumps up and finds place to get off ground (picnic table, chair, rock, swing.)

When 'it' says, "Go" everyone runs around play area.

'It' must "tig" or tag other players.

To be safe, players need to move their bodies off ground.

Basically, they find a safe base.

Players can only stay "off ground" for 1 minute.

Camp leader keeps time.

When minute has passed, players get down and run to another place where they can move "off the ground."

When player is "tigged," they are out.

Game ends when all players are out.

First player "tigged" becomes "it" for next game.

Get Moving Game: Snakes vs. Worms

Time:
Approx. 20 minutes

Materials Needed:
Green Yarn, Red Yarn, Scissors, Tape Measure or Yard Stick

Steps:

Cut green yarn (snake) and red yarn (worm) 20' long.

Larger groups may want to use 3 colors.

Cut each 20' strand into several smaller pieces.

Before play, camp leader hides pieces of yarn outside.

Form two teams (Worms vs. Snakes) with captains.

Team members go searching for worms or snakes.

When worms and snakes are found, captains tie each yarn piece to next.

Team with longest worm or snake wins.

Silly Game: Slurpin' for Worms

Time:
Approx. 15 minutes

Materials Needed:
Large Table, Paper Plates, Whipped Cream, Gummy Worms

Steps:
Line up the plates on table.

Two per player.

Add 5 worms to one plate, cover with whipped cream.

Leave other plate empty.

Players must place hands behind backs.

Players may use only mouths to find worms, one at a time, and spit them onto empty plate.

First player to find all 5 worms wins.

Tip: If playing one at a time, person with quickest time wins.

Do Monkey Around

Do Monkey Around (Designed for Campers 6-16.)

Planning Calendar

Song:
- *Monkeying Around*

Snacks:
- Crunchy Banana Pops

Arts & Crafts:
- Scratch and Sniff Paint
- Monkey Pencil Huggers

Science:
- Banana Experiments

Get Moving:
- Banana Relays
- Sensory Marshmallow Plop
- Cotton Ball Pick Up

Silly Game:
- Monkey, Monkey, Ape

Enrichment:
- Schedule a field trip to zoo or primate sanctuary.

SUN	MON	TUES	WED	THURS	FRI	SAT

Song to Sing: *Monkeying Around (Ooh ahh a a ahh)*

Ooh ahh a a ahh, monkeys eats bananas. (Pretend to peel banana.)

Ooh ahh a a ahh, just like you and me. (Point to each other.)

Ooh ahh a a ahh, monkeys swing on branches. (Pretend to hold branch and swing.)

Ooh ahh a a ahh, monkeys climb up trees. (Pretend to climb a tree.)

Ooh ahh a a ahh, monkeys scratch at fleas. (Pretend to scratch sides like a monkey.)

Ooh ahh a a ahh, monkeys walk on all fours. (Walk around circle like a monkey.)

Ooh ahh a a ahh. (Shout across circle.) Can you dance like a monkey?

(Shout back.) Ooh ahh a a ahh, I can- can you? (Dance like monkeys.)

Snack Activity: Crunchy Banana Pops

Time:
Approx. 15 minutes

Materials Needed:
Bananas, Vanilla Yogurt or Vanilla Pudding, ¼ C. Chopped Peanuts or ¼ C. Chocolate Pieces or ¼ C. Crushed Graham Crackers, Spoon, Wooden Craft Sticks - Measurements will make 2 pops.

Steps:

Peel banana, cut in half.

Put wooden stick in each banana half.

With spoon, spread yogurt or pudding lightly onto banana.

Roll banana into plate of chopped peanuts, chocolate pieces, or all three.

Roll banana in chocolate chips and graham cracker crumbs.

Art Activity: Scratch & Sniff Paint

Time:
Approx. 15 minutes

Materials Needed:
Neon Food Coloring, Milk, Cornstarch, Ice Cube Tray or Styrofoam Egg Box, Several Flavors of *Kool-Aid* Packets, Water Dropper, Tiny Mixing Spoon, Paint Brushes, White Paper, Salt, Maple Syrup (or Clear Corn Syrup)

Steps:

Mix three equal parts syrup, milk, and starch.

Add one or two drops of color.

Fill each square ½ full with *Kool-Aid* powder.

Add few drops of water into each square.

Mix with spoon until it looks like wet watercolor paint.

Paints should be fairly thick.

Add salt for shine and texture.

Campers can create greeting cards or use the paint on coloring pages.

For best results, allow art to dry overnight.

Next day, scratch and sniff.

Tip: Hang to dry with clothespins on clothesline.

Art Activity: Monkey Pencil Huggers

Time:
Approx. 15 minutes

Materials Needed:
Pencils, (3) Brown Pipe Cleaners, (1) Yellow Pipe Cleaner, Brown Plastic or Wooden Beads (1 larger for body), Googly Eyes, Tacky or Hot Glue, Brown Felt, Paint (for wooden beads)

Steps:

Start with 3 brown pipe cleaners, twist together in center to form star or firework shape. 1 in center with other two twisted at middle.

It is a 6 point star fanning out from middle pipe cleaner.

Top 3 pipe cleaner pieces form head and arms, bottom 3 pipe cleaner pieces form feet and tail.

Use larger bead, slide to middle where pipecleaners connect.

Bend 2 bottom pipe cleaner pieces to form legs and feet.

Wrap third bottom pipe cleaner around pencil to make spiral tail.

Bend 2 top pipe cleaner pieces to form hands and arms.

Tie knot in final pipe cleaner where it meets belly bead.

Loop pipe cleaner through hole in second bead.

Twist ends together, tuck into back of monkey.

Make banana by cutting small piece of yellow pipe cleaner.

Grab pencil, wrap hands around so it looks like he's hugging pencil.

Science Activity: Banana Experiments

Time:
Approx. 15 minutes

Materials Needed:
Bananas, Plastic Baggies

Steps:

Place one banana in refrigerator. Leave another banana on counter.

At end of week, compare bananas. What happened?

Overnight, place one banana in airtight container. Leave another banana on counter. What happened?

Gather five bananas and 3 baggies.

Place a RIPE banana in 1 baggie.

In second baggie, place 1 unripe banana.

In third baggie, place 2 unripe bananas.

Check baggies each day of camp.

Which bag over ripens first?

A ripe banana emits ethylene, this makes other bananas ripen.

Wrap banana in black bag, place in dark spot.

Keep banana under a lamp, don't let heat of light source touch banana.

What happened?

Get Moving Games: Banana Relays

Time:
Approx. 15 minutes

Materials Needed:
Bananas, Large Open Area (Marked with Start & Finish Line)

Steps:

Divide campers into teams, line up single file.

First relay: Place banana between knees, hop down course and back.

Tag next in line. Repeat until everyone has turn.

Second relay: 2 campers head down course tossing banana back and forth. Tag next in line.

Repeat until everyone has turn.

Third relay: Place banana under armpit, hop on one leg down and back.

Tag next in line.

Repeat until everyone has turn.

When done, collect bananas, peel them, and feed squirrels.

Silly Games: Sensory Marshmallow Plop

Time:
Approx. 15 minutes

Materials Needed:
Table, Mini-Marshmallows, Straws, Paper Cups, Timer

Steps:

Spread mini-marshmallows in center of tablecloth covered table.

Give each camper 1 cup and 1 straw.

Players use straw to pick up marshmallows.

No hands allowed.

Camp leader starts timer and says, "Ready, Set, Go!"

Suck on straw to pick up marshmallow, hold breath until dropped in cup.

When time is up, (1-2 minutes) count marshmallows that made it into cups.

Players with most marshmallows in cup wins.

Tip: For variation, fold straws in half and use as tool to pick up marshmallows.

Get Moving Game: Cotton Ball Straw Race

Time:
Approx. 15 minutes

Materials Needed:
Cotton Balls, Straws, Large Open Space, Masking Tape, Markers

Steps:

Set start and finish line with masking tape approx. 10' apart.

Mark different color dot on each cotton ball.

Give each player 1 straw and 1 cotton ball.

Players must move cotton ball from start to finish using only straw.

First to cross finish line wins.

Tip: Don't demonstrate how to play. Players can use straw like hockey stick, folded as chopsticks, or by blowing air toward cotton ball.

Silly Game: Monkey, Monkey, Ape

Time:
Approx. 15 minutes

Materials Needed:
Large Open Space

Steps:

Same game play as *Duck, Duck, Goose*, except when walking around circle, 'it' must move like a monkey.

Players sit down in circle, facing each other.

One person is 'it.'

'It' walks around outside of circle gently tapping each player on head and saying either "monkey" or "ape."

When player is tapped on head and called "ape," they stand up and chase 'it' around the outside of the circle, trying to catch and tag them.

The player making chase must act like ape.

If 'it' sits down in ape's spot before tagged, ape becomes 'it' and play continues.

If 'it' is tagged, 'it' continues to tap heads.

Sharks vs. Chickens

Sharks vs. Chickens (Designed for Campers 6-16.)

Planning Calendar

Song:
- *Funky Chicken and Baby Shark*

Snacks:
- Shark Teeth
- Chicken Feed

Arts & Crafts:
- Chicken Hat
- Shark Hat and Teeth

Science:
- Bouncing Eggs

Get Moving:
- What Time is it, Mr. Shark?
- Sharks, Roosters, and Hens

Silly Game:
- Animal Movements

Enrichment:
- Watch the movies, *"Sharkboy and Lavagirl"* and *"Chicken Run."*
- Take a Field Trip to an Aquarium or Family Farm.

SUN	MON	TUES	WED	THURS	FRI	SAT

Song to Song: *Funky Chicken*

Funky Chicken (make chicken motions)
Frankenstein (walk slowly with your arms out in front of you)
Ballerina (twirl and plié)
Sumo Wrestler (put hands on knees, bend, stomp feet one at a time)
Cleopatra (walk like an Egyptian)
Tree (put arms up like tree branches, stay still)
Elevator (pretend to push button on elevator, bend knees as if going down a floor, push button again. stand back up slowly)

LEADER: Let me see your funky chicken.
CAMPERS: What's that you say?
LEADER: I said, let me see your funky chicken.
CAMPERS: What's that you say?

EVERYONE: I said ooh ahh funky chicken, ooh ahh one more time, ooh ahh funky chicken, ooh ahh get back in line!

Funky Chicken (make chicken motions)
Frankenstein (walk slowly with your arms out in front of you)
Ballerina (twirl and plié)
Sumo Wrestler (put hands on knees, bend, stomp feet one at a time)
Cleopatra (walk like an Egyptian)
Tree (put arms up like tree branches, stay still)
Elevator (pretend to push button on elevator, bend knees as if going down a floor, push button again. stand back up slowly)

LEADER: Let me see your funky chicken.
CAMPERS: What's that you say?
LEADER: I said let me see your funky chicken.
CAMPERS: What's that you say?

EVERYONE: I said ooh ahh funky chicken, ooh ahh one more time, ooh ahh funky chicken, ooh ahh get back in line!

Song to Sing: *Baby Shark*

(Make shark mouth with two fingers)
Baby shark, do do do do do do
Baby shark, do do do do do do
Baby shark, do do do do do do Baby shark

(Make shark mouth with hands connected at wrist)
Mama shark, do do do do do do
Mama shark, do do do do do do
Mama shark, do do do do do do Mama shark

(Make shark mouth with whole arms)
Daddy shark, do do do do do do
Daddy shark, do do do do do do
Daddy shark, do do do do do do Daddy shark

(Make shark mouth with elbow)
Uncle shark, do do do do do do
Uncle shark, do do do do do do
Uncle shark, do do do do do do Uncle shark

(Make shark mouth like mama shark but with fists)
Grandma shark, ma ma ma ma ma ma
Grandma shark, ma ma ma ma ma ma
Grandma shark, ma ma ma ma ma ma Grandma shark

(Make swimming motion with arms)
Going swimming, do do do do do do
Going swimming, do do do do do do
Going swimming, do do do do do do Going swimming

(Make shark fin over head)
Sharks a'coming, do do do do do do
Sharks a'coming, do do do do do do
Sharks a'coming, do do do do do do Sharks a'coming

(Make swimming motion again, but faster)
Swimming faster, do do do do do do
Swimming faster, do do do do do do
Swimming faster, do do do do do do Swimming faster

(Make shark fin again, more frantic)

Sharks a'coming, do do do do do do

Sharks a'coming, do do do do do do

Sharks a'coming, do do do do do do Sharks a'coming

(All yell) SHARK ATTACK

(Make swimming motion with elbow)

Lost an arm, do do do do do do

Lost an arm, do do do do do do

Lost an arm, do do do do do do Lost an arm

(Put one hand on head like shark fin, other hand rubbing stomach)

Happy shark, do do do do do do

Happy shark, do do do do do do

Happy shark, do do do do do do Happy shark

(Make CPR motions)

CPR, do do do do do do

CPR, do do do do do do

CPR, do do do do do do CPR

(Make faster CPR motions)

It's not working, do do do do do do

It's not working, do do do do do do

It's not working, do do do do do do It's not working

(Fall to the floor)

Now you're dead.

Snack: Shark Teeth

Time:
Approx. 10 minutes

Materials Needed:
Bugles Snacks, Melted Queso Cheese

Steps:
Dip *Bugles* in melted queso cheese.

Tip: Make shark tooth necklace: http://briebrieblooms.com/shark-tooth-necklace-craft/

Snack: Chicken Feed

Time:
Approx. 25 minutes

Materials Needed:
3 ½ C. *Grape Nuts* Cereal, 1 C. Oatmeal, ¾ C. Peanut Butter (Check for Nut Allergies, can substitute with Almond or Sunflower Butter) ¾ C. Corn Syrup, ¼ C. Honey, 1 C. Sugar, 1 C. Peanuts (Omit if Allergies are Present) ½ C. White Chocolate Chips, 9 x 13 Pan, Butter or Cooking Spray, Microwave, Spoon, Spatula, Cutting Knife

Steps:

In large bowl, microwave corn syrup, honey, sugar, and peanut butter on high for 2 minutes.

Stir every 30 seconds.

Grease 9 x 13 pan with butter or cooking spray.

Remove bowl from microwave, stir in Grape Nuts, oatmeal, and peanuts.

Mix well, stir in the chocolate chips.

Pour into pan, spread with spatula.

Cut into bars.

Art Activity: Make a Chicken Hat

Companion Activity: Wear hat during shark vs. chicken games

Time:
Approx. 15 minutes

Materials Needed:
Red and Yellow Construction Paper, Scissors, Tape, Glue, Markers, Cardboard Cereal Boxes

Steps:

Cut 3, 2" strips down length of yellow construction paper.

Measure strip band to camper's head, glue or tape ends together for fit.

Fold strip in half to form chicken's beak.

Bend in half until ends meet, glue together, attach beak to hat band strip.

Cut red chicken wattle.

Paste wattle to beak, draw 2 black circles on beak for nostrils.

Cut 2 red paper "chicken combs" and glue to piece of cardboard to make comb stand tall.

Score slit in each end of comb, slide into hat band.

Tip: See it here:

https://www.kidscreativechaos.com/2013/04/how-to-make-rooster-or-chicken-hat-band.html

Art Activity: Make a Shark Hat

Companion Activity: Wear hat during shark vs. chicken games

Time:
Approx. 15 minutes

Materials Needed:
Blue and White Construction Paper, Scissors, Tape, Glue, Markers, Cardboard Cereal Boxes

Steps:

Cut 3, 2" strips down length of blue construction paper.

Measure strip band to camper's head, glue or tape ends together for fit.

Attach final strip across top, like a hat.

Cut shark fin from blue paper and cardboard.

With tape, attach fin to top headband strip.

Tip: For reference, see chicken headband here:
https://www.kidscreativechaos.com/2013/04/how-to-make-rooster-or-chicken-hat-band.html

Art Activity: Make Shark Jaws

Time:

Approx. 15 minutes

Materials Needed:

Scissors, Tape, Paper or Styrofoam Plates (*Chinet* Plates work best)

Steps:

Fold plate in half, backward.

With scissors, trim small circle from center of plate.

This makes it easier to cut out teeth.

Keep plate folded in half, cut jagged teeth triangles all around semi-circle.

Tip: See sample here:

https://boingboing.net/2012/02/27/howto-make-shark-jaws-out-of-p.html

Science Activity: Bouncing Eggs

Time:

Approx. 3 days

Materials Needed:
Boiled Egg, Raw Egg, White Vinegar. Large Bowl, Outdoor Space

Steps:

Place boiled egg in bowl.

Completely cover egg with vinegar.

After three days, remove egg from bowl.

Rinse shell off egg.

Go outside, bounce egg.

Try it with raw egg too.

Tip: See it here:
https://www.kidscreativechaos.com/2016/03/science-things-to-do-with-eggs-includes.html

Extra Shark Experiments:

https://www.connectionsacademy.com/resources/instructographics/shark-science-activity

https://jdaniel4smom.com/2017/07/stem-shark-activities-for-kids-how-sharks-float.html

Get Moving Game: What Time is it Mr. Shark
(adapted from *What Time is it Mr. Wolf*)

Time:
Approx. 15 minutes

Materials Needed:
Large Open Space, Shark Hat, Start/Finish Line

Steps:
Play is similar to *Red Light, Green Light*. Instead of one person calling out red light or green light, shark responds to question,"What's the time, Mr. Shark?" by calling out different times. Camper is chosen as shark. He stands with back toward others, who stand approximately 20' behind start line. Together, campers shout, "What's the Time, Mr. Shark?" Shark turns around, faces players answering with a time. For example, eight o'clock. Time shark chooses is number of steps players take toward shark. For example, eight o'clock = eight steps forward. Then, shark turns back waiting for campers to ask again. Play continues until shark thinks campers are close enough to catch. When close, shark responds to "What's the Time, Mr. Shark?" with "Dinnertime!" Shark chases campers to tag one before they make it back to start line. When camper is tagged before crossing start line, player becomes shark. If all campers make it back across start line without being tagged, shark continues to try to catch one.

Get Moving Game: Simple Capture the Flag

Time:
Approx. 20 minutes

Materials Needed:
Large Open Space, 2 Flags (Bandanas), Designated Boundaries, Space for Penalty

Steps:

Object of game is to grab other team's flag and carry it safely back to safety zone. Divide into Shark and Chicken teams.

Discuss designated boundaries.

Flag must be visible, place 1 flag in back pocket or pant's waist of 1 player from each team.

Part of each team guards flag bearer, part of each team tries to capture opposing team's flag.

Players may not trip other players, nor can they use hands to stop them.

Players can dance in front of players and block by standing near flag.

If player touches another player, they must sit in penalty box (sidelines.)

To win game, player who captures flag must make it back to their team's safe zone without getting tagged.

Get Moving Game: Sharks, Hens, and Roosters
(adapted from *Monsters, Elves, and Wizards*)

Time:
Approx. 20 minutes

Materials Needed:
Large Open Space, Jump Ropes, Whistle

Steps:

Hens: Beat Sharks. *Action:* Hens scratch feet on ground, flap wings, (elbows) pretend to peck at opposing team.

Roosters: Beat Hens. *Action:* Roosters flap wings, cockadoodle-doo.

Sharks: Beat Roosters. *Action:* Sharks put hands over heads to make fins, walk in squiggly line (swim.)

Decide on boundaries, use jump rope to mark center line.

Campers divide into 2 teams.

Camp Leader is referee.

Each team huddles together, decides which character to portray.

Camp Leader blows whistle to start play.

Teams start acting like chosen character.

Winning team's character chases other team members to tag out.

Play continues until one team captures all members of other team.

Silly Game: Animal Movements

Time:
Approx. 15 minutes

Materials Needed:
Large Open Space

Steps:

Sit or stand in circle.

Choose one person to start moving like animal.

No sounds allowed.

Campers try to guess animal.

When guessed correctly, all move like that animal.

Person who guessed correctly starts new animal movement.

Daily Time Fillers

Additional Daily Time Fillers
- More Camp Snacks
- Edible Paint Recipes
- Songs
    - Boom Boom
    - Do your Ears Hang Low?
- More Games
    - Ha Ha Ha
    - Honey if You Love Me
    - This is a What
    - Cotton Ball Relay
    - Cotton Ball Target Drop

More Snacks to Make

Yogurt Pop Ice Cubes
https://www.kidscreativechaos.com/2015/06/yogurt-ice-cube-snacks-recipe.html

Character Biscuit Pizza Poppers
https://www.kidscreativechaos.com/2015/09/grands-halloween-recipe-easy-edible-art.html

Frozen Pudding Pops
https://www.kidscreativechaos.com/2015/07/homemade-pudding-pops-recipe.html

Jumping Jellyfish
https://www.kidscreativechaos.com/2015/08/school-lunch-bag-ideas.html

Easy Shape Pizzas
https://www.kidscreativechaos.com/2016/02/heart-shaped-pizza-without-yeast.html

Edible Paint Recipes

Paint Recipe: Easy Pudding Paint

Time:

Approx. 5 minutes

Materials Needed:
Vanilla Pudding Snack Cups, Gel Food Coloring, Swirling Stick or Spoon

Steps:

Open pudding cup.

Add 3-4 drops gel food coloring.

Stir with stick.

Coconut Oil Face Paint
https://www.kidscreativechaos.com/2016/08/non-toxic-face-paint-homemade-recipe.html

Milk Paint
https://www.kidscreativechaos.com/2009/02/paint-heart-on-your-toast-for.html

Salt and Flour Paint
https://tinkerlab.com/salt-and-flour-paint/

Song to Sing: Boom Boom Ain't it Great to be Crazy

Boom boom ain't it great to be crazy?

Boom boom ain't it great to be crazy?

Silly and foolish the whole day through

Boom boom ain't it great to be crazy?

Way down south where bananas grow

A flea stepped on an elephant's toe

The elephant cried, with tears in his eyes

"Why don't you pick on someone your own size?"

Way up north where there's ice and snow

There was a penguin and his name was Joe

He got tired of black and white

So he wore pink pants to the dance last night!

A horse and a flea and three blind mice

Sat on the curbstone shooting dice

The horse, he slipped and fell on the flea

Boom boom ain't it great to be crazy?

Song to Sing: Do Your Ears Hang Low

Do Your Ears Hang Low?

Do They Wobble to and Fro?

Can You Tie Them in a Knot?

Can You Tie Them in a Bow?

Can You Throw Them Over Your Shoulder Like a Continental Soldier?

Do Your Ears Hang Low?

Do Your Ears Hang High?

Do They Reach Up to the Sky?

Do The Droop When They're Wet?

Do They Stiffen When They're Dry?

Can You Semaphore Your Neighbor with a Minimum of Labor?

Do Your Ears Hang High?

Do Your Ears Hang Wide?

Do They Flap From Side to Side?

Do They Wave in the Breeze?

From the Slightest Little Sneeze?

Can You Soar Above the Nation with a Feeling of Elation?

Do Your Ears Hang Wide?

Do Your Ears Fall Off?

When You Give a Great Big Cough?

Do They Lie There on the Ground?

Or Bounce Up at Every Sound?

Can You Stick Them in Your Pocket Just Like Little Davy Crockett?

Do Your Ears Fall Off?

Tip: For More songs like this visit our website: https://www.kidscreativechaos.com/2015/07/circle-activities-for-teens-middle.html

Silly Game: Ha Ha Ha!

Time:

Approx. 10 minutes

Materials Needed:
Large Open Space

Steps:

Everyone lies in circle with head on neighbor's stomach.

On 'go,' first person shouts 'HA' then one by one, clockwise around circle, all take turns repeating.

All heads bounce up on other person's stomach when 'HA' is shouted.

Next, shout two 'HA HAs' and go around again.

Continue doing this increasing number of 'HAs' each go around.

Goal: Get up to 10 'HA HAs.'

Silly Game: Honey if You Love Me…

Time:

Approx. 10 minutes

Materials Needed:
Large Open Space

Steps:

Group starts in circle with one person in middle.

Middle player tries to get others to laugh by saying "Honey if you love me, you'll smile."

Player on outside must respond without smiling or laughing, saying, "Honey, I love you, but I just can't smile."

Middle player does various things without touching other person to get a smile.

If person in middle smiles, players trade places.

Silly Game: This is a What?

Time:
Approx. 10 minutes

Materials Needed:
Large Open Space, Several Objects to Pass (Dolls, Cars, Balls, Shoes, etc.)

Steps:

Group sits in circle.

Leader starts by looking to person next to him and holding up object in his hand. For example, a doll. He says, "This is a doll."

She responds, "A what?"

He says, "A doll."

She says "A what?"

He says, "A shoe."

She takes the doll and says, "oh, a doll."

She turns to next person and starts same interaction. Leader adds more items into mix, starting the same way, joining into same rhythm already established by doll.

Goal: Have as many items going around as people in circle. Players are turning to one person and saying what an item is while saying "a what" to other person at same time.

Get Moving Game: Cotton Ball Relay

Time:

Approx. 15 minutes

Materials Needed:
Large Open Space, Cotton Balls, 4 Large Bowls, Blindfold, Wooden Spoons, Masking Tape

Steps:

Divide into teams.

Line up single file.

Put tape on floor to create start line.

For each team, place bowl of 10 cotton balls at start line and bowl 15' away.

On 'go,' first player from each team takes spoon, scoops up cotton ball, and walks down to bowl on other end dropping ball in bowl.

When player drops cotton ball into bowl, he races back to start and tags next player to go.

If cotton ball falls off spoon, player must return and start over.

No hands allowed.

First team to empty start bowl and fill finish bowl wins.

Get Moving Game: Cotton Ball Target Drop

Time:

Approx. 15 minutes

Materials Needed:
Large Open Space, Cotton Balls, Large Bowl, Step Stool

Steps:

Place bowl on floor.

Give each player 5 cotton balls.

First player stands on step stool.

Player holds cotton ball to nose, lets drop into bowl below.

Each player gets 5 tries.

Player with most balls in bowl wins.

Forms & Registration

Forms & Registrations

- Typical Schedule (Sample)
- Printable Daily Activity Schedule
- Printable Snack Menu
- Blank Calendar
- Printable Birthday Poster
- Sample Parent Letter
- Sample Camp Flyer
- Camp Registration Forms
    - Weekly Camper Registration
    - Waivers
    - Medical/Allergy Info Sheet
    - Photo/Media Permission

Typical Camp at Home Schedule

730	Early Arrival (Board Games, Quiet Activities)
800	Welcome, Icebreaker, Camp Motto, and Morning Snack
830	Recreational Play (Outdoor Games)
900	Water & Bathroom Break
915	Circle Group Game
945	Science
1015	Free Play (Choice of Outdoor Activities)
1045	Water & Bathroom Break
1100	**Lunch**
1120	Circle Group Game
1140	Technology Time
1200	Recreational Play (Outdoor Games)
1230	Water Break
1235	Arts & Crafts
100	Circle Counselor Rap Time
115	Special Guest Enrichment Program
215	Water & Bathroom Break
230	Afternoon Snack (Freezer Pops)
245	Science
315	Free Play
345	Recreational Play (Outdoor Games)
415	Arts & Crafts
445	Circle Group Game/Counselor Rap Time
500	Regular Pick Up/Late Stays (Board Games or Movie)
530	Late Pick Up

TODAY'S ACTIVITIES

SNACKS

Monday

Tuesday

Wednesday

Thursday

Friday

SUN	MON	TUES	WED	THURS	FRI	SAT

Hip Hip Hooray!

HAPPY BIRTHDAY

_ _ _ _ _ _ _ _ _ _ _ _ _ _

Sample Parent Letter

Camp Muddy Socks
Sandy's House
1234 W. 0th Street, Summerville FL
(317) 123-4567

Dear Summer Camp Parent:

Welcome to *Camp Muddy Socks* Summer Camp Week #1 - June.

This letter gives IMPORTANT information. Please read carefully.

NECESSARY MUMBO JUMBO

Parents are responsible for the following:

Payment is due the Friday **before** attendance. If not paid by Monday at 5:30 p.m. you will be required to pay a $5 per day late fee. If payment is not received by the following Friday, your child will not be allowed to attend future camp days.

Parents MUST sign children in and out. No Exceptions.

Pick-up person is required to show I.D. to site leader until all staff recognize all pick up people. Please be patient, this is for the security of your child.

Children will not be released to anyone not listed as designated pick up person.

Immunizations must be current. We must have a copy on file by June 1. After this date, the child will not be allowed to attend camp until records are current.

The program operates 7:30-5:30 p.m. daily. Prior to any late pick-up you may purchase a late pick-up pass which allows pick-ups until 5:45 p.m. This pass is $20 per week per family. No pick ups are allowed after this time. A staff member is on duty for clean-up until 6:00 p.m. No staff member has the authority to authorize pickups past 5:45, doing so will jeopardize their position and the integrity of the program.

This is for the safety of your child, as well as the staff, and prevents any one from being left alone in a one-on-one situation. Also, if a staff member allows parents to become accustomed to the service and is not on duty every day, it could produce an awkward situation.

Please do not ask Staff to bend the rules. If you are running late due to unforeseen circumstances such as car trouble, please call ahead to inform the staff. There is a $1.00 per minute late fee paid directly to staff on duty. Emergencies are not an exception to this rule.

It is against *Camp Muddy Socks* policy for staff to babysit outside of program hours. If you need evening or weekend childcare, please notify the Program Director. We are happy to recommend a babysitter, as well as, approve a staff member to serve you. You will negotiate the fee.

Please do not ask a staff member to babysit without prior approval. You are jeopardizing the safety of our program and the safety of your children. Any staff member found to babysit without approval will be dismissed without question. This may sound unnecessarily harsh, unfortunately in today's society, it is necessary to safeguard your children.

On a similar note, no staff member is allowed to transport your child home. The legal consequences are astounding and too numerous to mention. Please do not ask. Again, if you have a prior, personal relationship with a staff member who is willing and you approve to drive your child home please notify the Program Director. You will be required to fill out a permission slip waiving your rights to litigation against *Camp Muddy Socks* should an unforeseen incident occur. The staff member will also have to sign a waiver. We take every measure to insure the safety of children in our care.

Thank you for your patience and acknowledgement of the above rules. **Now, let's get to the fun Mumbo Jumbo!**

Our program is loosely structured. We have many similar views to the Montessori style of teaching. While we follow a schedule, it is flexible. If an activity is taking longer than expected and the children are enjoying themselves, we will continue. If half-way through a scheduled activity, all children are in agreement that it is not fun, we will move on to the next activity ahead of schedule.

Likewise, we believe children should have choices. If they do not wish to participate in a particular activity they may choose one of the following options:

> Read a book.
> Color a picture.
> Take a nap.

However, this MUST take place in the same location as the rest of the group.

Many of our activities will be large group to help maintain the safety and sustainability for all involved.

It may often appear chaotic to some who are not used to being around groups of children. Organized chaos is a great tool to make structure seem fun! Our patient staff is comfortable with the activity level and noise. If a staff member ever seems stressed, please pass this info along to the Program Director. Email is an excellent way to communicate and keep a record of our discussion.

Thank you so much for your patronage and support of our rules.

Sincerely,

Sandy Momathome, *Camp Muddy Socks* After School

Sample Camp Flyer

Let's Play!

Monkey Business
Full & Half-Day Summer Camps
(18 mos. - 11 yrs.)

Do Monkey Around!
Come act silly with us! We'll paint our faces like monkeys, make masks, read a story and pretend we've gone bananas in a jungle! 18 -36 mos. Parents welcome to stay & participate.

T/W/TH, June 15 - 17 9:30 - 10:05 a.m. $20/Siblings $15

Funky Monkeys
Make monkey faces and masks for a very silly monkey skit. Pretend you're a monkey while exploring a hiking trail in the woods and play outside on the playground. 2 ½ -5 yrs. Sack Lunch required.

T/W/TH, June 15 - 17 10:30 - 2:30 p.m. $60/Siblings $35

Manic Monkeys
Shake those sillies out and go bananas! Learn to paint monkey faces on your friends. Practice silly monkey comedy on stage and act out a play about Monkeys! Lots of outdoor playtime and scavenger hunts in the parks trails. 5-11 yrs. (Must have completed kindergarten.) Sack Lunch required.

M/T/W/TH, June 14 - 17 (8:30 a.m. - 4:30 p.m.) $75/Siblings $50

Early Arrival 7:30-8:30 a.m. $5/Late Departure 4:30-6:00 p.m. $15

CAMP Registration Form

Camp Muddy Socks

Come play with us this summer. Enjoy 5 Fun Filled Weeks of Camp.

Monday-Friday, 8:00 - 5:00 ($99)
Extended Care: 7:15-8 a.m. ($15) & 5-6:15 p.m. ($10)

(Field Trips & Enrichment programs may incur additional fees.)

Child's Name: _____

Age: _____

Parent's Email:
_____

Parent's Name/Phone:
_____

Authorized Pick-up Person:
_____

Allergies:
_____

Pay by Check/Cash/Paypal/Credit. We'll send an email invoice for Paypal/Credit Card payments.

email:_____

Last Name: _____   Date: ___/___/____

CHILD REGISTRATION FORM

PROGRAM

5-Day Camp   Half-Day Camp   Drop N Go   Class   Special Event

Child's Name:

_____

Parent/Guardian:

_____

Address:

_____

_____

Home/Mobile: _____ Work: _____

Authorized Pick Up Person (s):

_____

Home/Mobile: _____ Work: _____

Emergency Medical Info:

_____

Please list any SPECIAL NEEDS your child may have on the back of this form. Including food or insect allergies.

Doctor: _____ Phone: _____

Emergency Medical Release: If an emergency occurs and I cannot be contacted, I authorize the staff to grant permission for my child to receive emergency medical treatment. Initials: _____

Parent Contract: I understand and agree to the following: To pick up my child at designated time or pay $5 for every 15 minutes late after 2 p.m. and $1 per every minute late after 6 p.m. I will sign my child in and out everyday with camp staff. If attending camp, I will provide a daily sack lunch. If attending Drop N Shop and my child is not potty trained I will provide "Pull-Ups." All Camp fees are due in advance, my child is not officially registered until payment is received and there are no refunds. Any payments made in advance and not used can be applied to any of the programs. Furthermore, I agree to hold harmless _____ (Fill in Camp Director and Camp Name) and all of its employees should an unforeseen accident occur.

Signature: _____

Date: _____/_____/_____

Photography/Media Release:

I hereby give my child permission to be included in any media publicity coverage.

Parent/Guardian Signature:

_____

REGISTRATION FORM

Please circle the day you wish to attend:

Tuesday   Wednesday   Thursday

Child's Name:
_____

Parent/Guardian:
_____

Email Address:
_____

Home/Mobile: _____ Work:_____

Photography/Media Release

I hereby give my child permission to be included in any media publicity coverage.

Parent/Guardian Signature:
_____

Sample Camp Weekly Registration

Registration for *Camp Muddy Socks* Day Camp

Circle the weeks the camper is attending and tally all totals. Please fill out form completely and return to: 12345 Suite 101, E. U.S. HWY 123, Sumerville, FL 00123 or fax to 317-123-4567. Forms can also be emailed. If you have any questions please call.

Week	Theme	Fee	Early Arrival	Late Depart	T-shirt	Total
May 26-29 (T-F)	Cars Wheeled Racers	85	10	15	7	117
June 2-4	Surf's Up Beach Volleyball	75	10	15	7	
June 9-11	Mighty Ducks Hockey Sticks	75	10	15	7	
June 16-18	Bad News Bears Ball	75	10	15	7	
June 23-25	A Bug's Life Soccer	75	10	15	7	
June 30-2	Air Bud Basketball	75	10	15	7	
July 7-9	Kangaroo Jack Kickball	75	10	15	7	

Camper Name:
Cash/Check - Circle one. *A $35 charge applies to all NSF checks.
Credit Card VISA /MASTERCARD /DISCOVER - Circle one. Name on card: _____ Card # Expiration / /
Parent Contract I understand and agree to the following: To pick up my child at designated time or pay $1.00 per minute late fee. I will sign my child in and out everyday with camp staff. I will provide a daily sack lunch for my child. I understand that the first week's payment is required as deposit upon registration & fees paid up front can be applied to future weeks. There are no refunds. My child is not officially registered until payment is received. All fees are due in advance & my child may not stay at camp without payment in full. Initials _____ Date__/__/__ **Photography/Media Release:** I hereby give my child permission to be included in any media publicity coverage. _____ Parent/Guardian Signature
**T-shirts are optional. Please circle appropriate size when ordering. YS YM YL AS AL AXL
This part to be completed by Camp Staff: PIF Y/N Waiver signed Y/N Multiple Weeks Y/N Special Needs Y/N

NOTES

Made in the USA
Lexington, KY
30 May 2019